2024
vision board
CLIP ART BOOK

500+elements
BY KALISHIA WINSTON

YOUR FREE GIFTS

As a way of saying thanks for your purchase,
I want to offer you two free bonuses:

FREE GIFT #1:

"86 QUICK & EASY STRATEGIES FOR SAVING MONEY" EBOOK

Discover 86 practical and easy-to-implement strategies to save money, budget wisely, and achieve your financial goals. This eBook is a valuable resource for securing your financial future.

FREE GIFT #2:

"CREATING YOUR DREAM LIFE WITH YOUR OWN VISION BOARD" COURSE

Unlock the potential within you and start manifesting your aspirations with my exclusive vision board course. Set clear intentions and turn your dreams into reality.

SIGN UP FOR MY EMAIL NEWSLETTER TO GET INSTANT ACCESS:
2024.KALISHIAWINSTON.COM

You will also get weekly tips, free book giveaways, discounts, and so much more.

All of these bonuses are completely free and come with no strings attached. You do not need to provide any personal information except for your email address.

2024 NEW START

MAKE THIS A YEAR TO REMEMBER

2024

DREAM BIG!

2024 - THE YEAR OF VICTORY

2024 RESOLUTIONS

2024 NEW YEAR GOALS

365 NEW DAYS 365 NEW CHANCES

2024

FULL POWER YEAR!

❗ TOP PRIORITIES IN 2024

1	
2	
3	
4	
5	
6	
7	
8	
9	
10	

✪ THINGS TO ACCOMPLISH IN 2024

1	
2	
3	
4	
5	
6	
7	
8	
9	
10	

⚙ SKILLS TO DEVELOP IN 2024

1	
2	
3	
4	
5	
6	
7	
8	
9	
10	

📖 BOOKS TO READ IN 2024

1	
2	
3	
4	
5	
6	
7	
8	
9	
10	

📍 PLACES TO TRAVEL IN 2024

1	
2	
3	
4	
5	
6	
7	
8	
9	
10	

♟ THINGS TO LEARN IN 2024

1	
2	
3	
4	
5	
6	
7	
8	
9	
10	

🍴 FOODS TO TRY IN 2024

1	
2	
3	
4	
5	

🍽 RESTAURANTS TO VISIT IN 2024

1	
2	
3	
4	
5	

DO YOGA

TAKE TIME TO
REFRESH
RELAX
RESTART

Mindfulness

find your
inner peace

Meditation

Mind
Body
Soul

BE KIND
TO YOUR
MIND

RUN!

ENERGY Be Active!

8725
MARATHON

WORRY LESS RUN MORE

BAD WEATHER
IS NOT AN EXCUSE
IT'S COMPETITION

WALK
EVERY
DAY

10000 STEPS DAILY

EXERCISE REGULARLY

WINNERS NEVER QUIT AND QUITTERS NEVER WIN

SPORT IS A PRESERVER OF HEALTH
HIPPOCRATES

LOSE

POUNDS

MORNING ROUTINE

self-care shouldnt be rare

Take care of yourself

DIGITAL DETOX

MEN NEED SELF CARE TOO

SELF CARE

ISN'T SELFISH

SELF ♡ CARE

NO DAY WITHOUT LEARNING

GOAL SETTING

MENTORING

ENTREPRENEUR
HUSTLE | GRIND | EXECUTE

SMALL *business*

C.E.O

DELEGATE TASKS

WELCOME
WE ARE
OPEN
PLEASE COME IN

Choose a JOB YOU Love AND YOU WILL NEVER Have to WORK A DAY IN YOUR Life

WORK FROM HOME

DREAM OFFICE

Business Plan

DIGITAL NOMAD

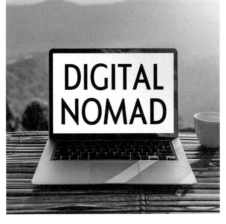

ONLINE STORE

DEBT-FREE

PASSIVE INCOME

BUDGET PLAN

1.
2.
3.
4.
5.
6.

FINANCIAL FREEEDOM

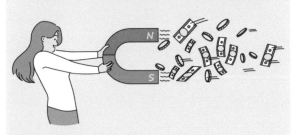

I am a MONEY MAGNET

Multiple Income Streams

Spend less than you earn!

NO IMPULSE BUYING

HARMONY
SERENITY

FREEDOM DREAM**CAR**

MOVIE NIGHT

I love you!!!

DRIVE-IN THEATER

DATE NIGHT

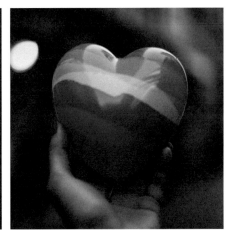

BUILDING DREAMS TOGETHER

Making **MEMORIES**

UNCONDITIONAL LOVE

LOVE IS THE ANSWER

Embracing a Future Perfect Moment
TOGETHER
♡A Proposal to Remember

SHE SAID Yes!

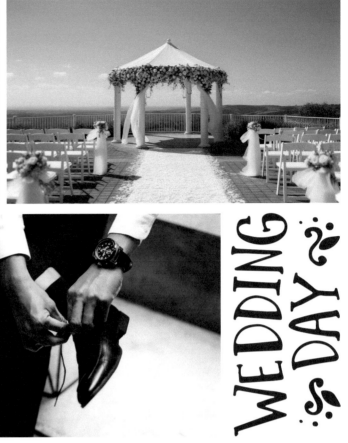

BABY NAME

MOM EST. 2024

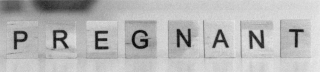

PREGNANT

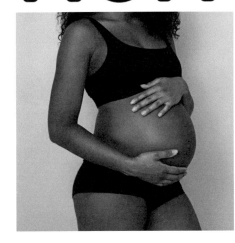
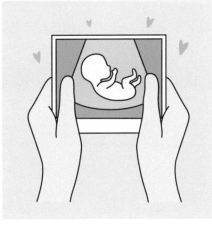
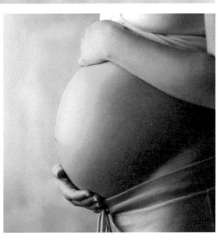

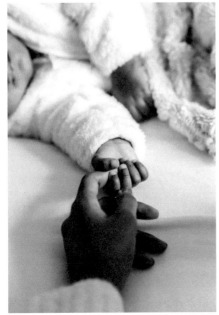

BABY

GUIDING LITTLE HEARTS

friendship

Shared Moments

#UNBREAKABLEBOND

Heartfelt Empathy

Declutter   Keep

SIMPLIFY

Clear Mind, Clear Space

EMBRACE MINIMALISM

Get ORGANIZED

parrot

GUINEA PIG **Hamster**

time spent with **Dogs**

CAT MOM

Wanderlust

LIFE IS A *Journey*

READY •FOR new• ADVENTURES

ENJOY
THE NATURE

green mind

ZERO WASTE

Nature

Go to nature and you
will feel free.

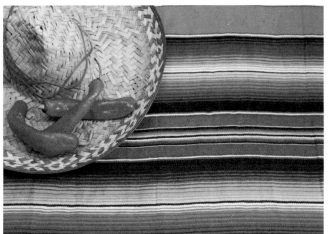

Millionaire LIFESTYLE *Abundance*

✈ BOARDING PASS

FROM: TO:

PASSENGER NAME:

⟶

_____

BOARDING TIME: DATE:

_____

SEAT: FLIGHT:

_____

For manifesting purposes only. Not for use to board a flight at the airport.

🏛 BANK OF THE UNIVERSE

DATE: _____

PAY TO THE
ORDER OF: _____

$ _____

_____ DOLLARS

FOR: _____

00000000 156   00000000 296 456

For manifesting purposes only.

SPECIAL TICKET
VIP GUEST

Event:

Exclusively for:

For the sole purpose of manifesting your desires.

Date:
Location:

ADMIT ONE VIP GUEST
VIP PASS

Name:

Company:

Title:

📞

✉

📍

GOLD MEMBER

VIP Club Name

Name

member no.
123-456-789

Inspire

Smile

BE GOOD, DO GOOD.

good things take time.

be yourself

GET IT DONE

KNOW YOUR **WORTH**

Good Vibes

CHASE Goals

Dream it. Believe it. Achieve it...

Just keep moving forward.

if you **NEVER TRY** you will **NEVER KNOW**

STRIVE FOR GREATNESS.

MAKE EVERYDAY **WORTH** LIVING >>>>>

YOUR *attitude* DETERMINES YOUR *direction*

YOU CAN DO ANYTHING

Difficult roads often lead to *Beautiful* destination

DON'T *yourself* **QUIT.**

CHOOSE HAPPY

PERFECTION **PROGRESS**

LIFE IS SO **GOOD**

LIVE LOVE LAUGH

Ambitious

Auspicious

Authentic

Brave

Confident

Determined

Dreaming

Empowered

Fearless

Fighter

Flawless

Glamorous

Grateful

Happiness

Harmonious

Hustle

Motivated

Perfection

be kind to ME

Feel Good

drink more water

eat healthy

be a good friend

MEDITATE

put the past in the past

ENJOY NATURE

find a new hobby

GET A NEW JOB

BE DEBT FREE

start a side hustle

Watch Less TV

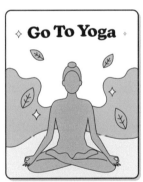
Go To Yoga

Save Money

MAKE NEW FRIENDS

Less Screen Time

sleep more

get better grades

LAUGH OUT LOUD

PAY IT FORWARD

get organized

be mindful

learn to cook

Listen Actively

Read More Books

TRAVEL MORE

find balance

be optimistic

Get Creative

Gardening

Get Fit

Prioritize Sleep

work hard, play hard

Relax More

PRIORITISE HEALTH

THANK YOU

"Helping others is the way we help ourselves."
-Oprah Winfrey

Have you ever given without expecting anything in return? If you have, you are aware of the tremendous rewards that can come from helping others. Not because it makes you a better person, but because it makes you feel good to know that you were able to improve someone else's life in some small way.

I want to give you this chance and ask you for a favor. In order for me to accomplish my mission of inspiring my readers to live their best lives, I first have to reach them. And the majority of people do evaluate a book based on its reviews. So, could you please take 3 minutes to post your honest review of this book on Amazon? With your help, this book will reach more people and assist them in achieving their goals and dreams. Just find this book on Amazon and write a few short words (or long words, I won't judge).

P.S. If you believe this book will benefit someone you know, please let them know about it too.

To your success,

Kalishia Winston

Made in United States
Troutdale, OR
04/18/2024